IDIA
of the Benin Kingdom
Coloring and Activity Book

Copyright © 2020 Our Ancestories

All rights reserved. No part of this publication may be reproduced, distributed, or transmitted in any form or by any means, including photocopying, recording, or other electronic or mechanical methods, without the prior written permission of the publisher, except in the case of brief quotations embodied in critical reviews and certain other noncommercial uses permitted by copyright law.

ISBN: 978-1-7771179-3-1 (Paperback)

First Print Edition

www.our-ancestories.com

Follow Your Dreams

Coloring: Idia had a dream about a woman fighting in a raging battle. Later on, she had another dream that she was that woman. In that dream, she was a queen and had a young son who was a king. She dreamed that the enemy was attacking the kingdom. No wonder Idia wanted to learn about being a warrior and being protected by the gods and medicine. Color Idia and the designs.

The Friends Running to the Festival

A Maze: Idia and her friend Adesuwa ran through the rainforest to get to the Igue festival, a day of celebration in the village of Ugieghudu. Help Idia and Adesuwa through the maze to the Igue Festival.

My favorite activity is dancing!
What's yours?
Can you write about it or draw a picture?

The Edo Language

Word Puzzle. Use the clues to spell the words used in the story. (The first letter of each word is capitalized to help you.)

1. King   b O a   _____

2. Drum   m E a   _____

3. Father   a h E r   _____

4. Mother   y I e   _____

5. God   b s n o O a a u _____

6. Guardian Angel   i h E   _____

7. Queen Mother   b y I o a   _____

Everyone Has Chores

A Maze. The villagers had many chores. Idia danced and entertained everyone. Mother used her knowledge of herbs to help people heal. Father was the protector of the family. He knew how to use weapons. Help Idia and her parents find their way through the maze.

"One of my dreams was to be a warrior. To become one, I practiced with my dad."

What are your dreams?
What will you do to make them happen?

Creative Writing. Write about your dreams. Use at least 3 complete sentences.

....
....
....
....
....
....
....
....
....
....
....

*Younger children can dictate their ideas, and an adult can do the writing for them.

The Edo Language

Crossword Puzzle. Complete the puzzle. Use the Edo language that the Benin people speak for the given clues.

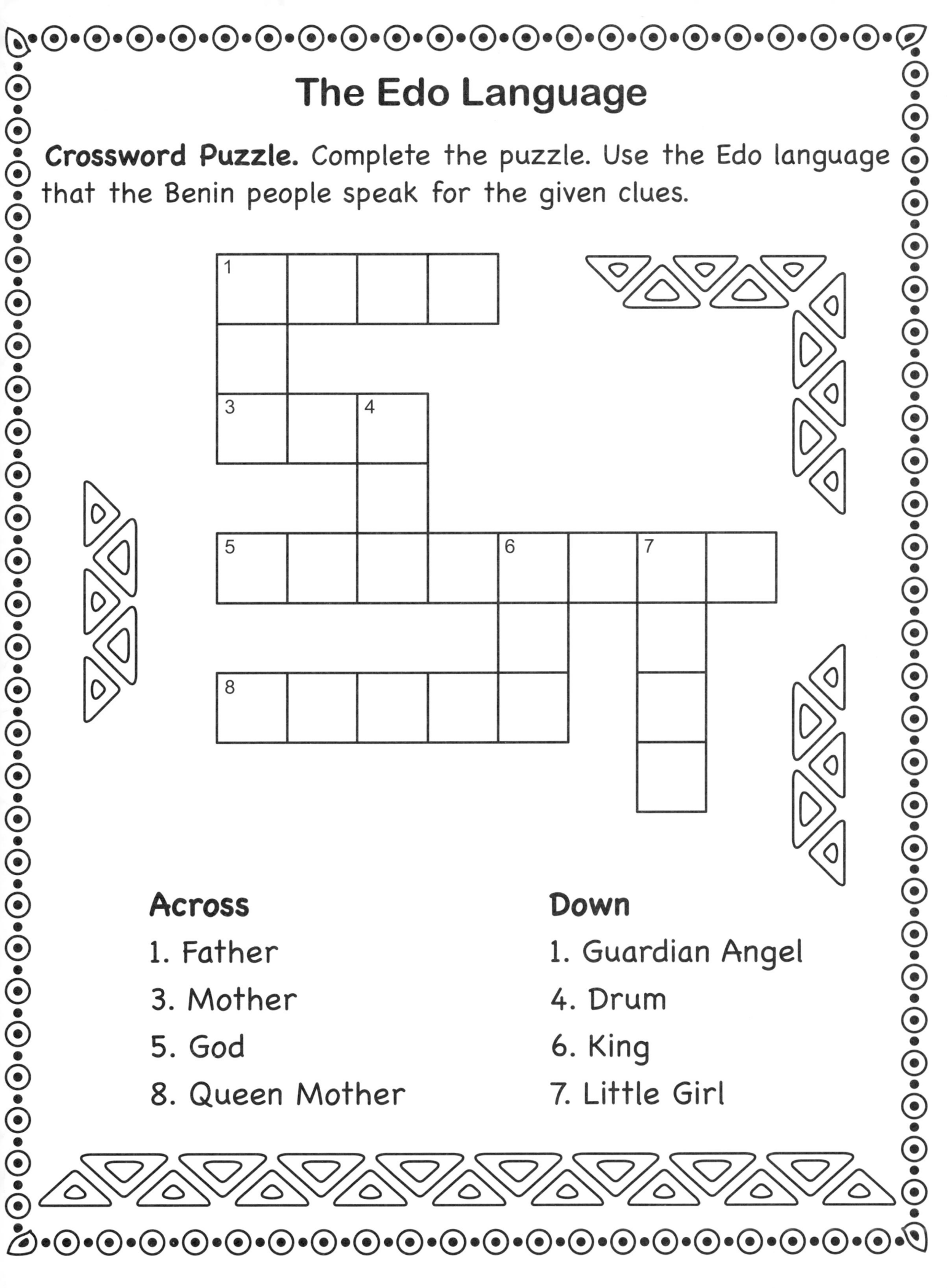

Across
1. Father
3. Mother
5. God
8. Queen Mother

Down
1. Guardian Angel
4. Drum
6. King
7. Little Girl

Idia Asks Her Mother

A Maze. Idia always wanted to learn more about plants and healing, magic, and medicine. Her mother finally agreed to teach her. Mother told Idia to keep doing her chores. Then she would teach Idia about the gods and medicine. Help Idia find her way through the maze to her mother.

Story Concepts

Crossword Puzzle. Complete the puzzle with the listed words from the story.

Use these words: Adesuwa, Igue, enemy, healing, warrior, kingdom, dance, dreams, weapons, Idia

Across

2. first Queen Mother of Benin
5. those opposed in time of war
7. a day of celebration in the village
8. thoughts and images in a person's mind while sleeping
9. an area of land ruled by a king or queen

Down

1. a brave or experienced fighter
3. Idia's friend
4. the process of being healthy again
6. things used to defend in conflict
8. a performing art of movement

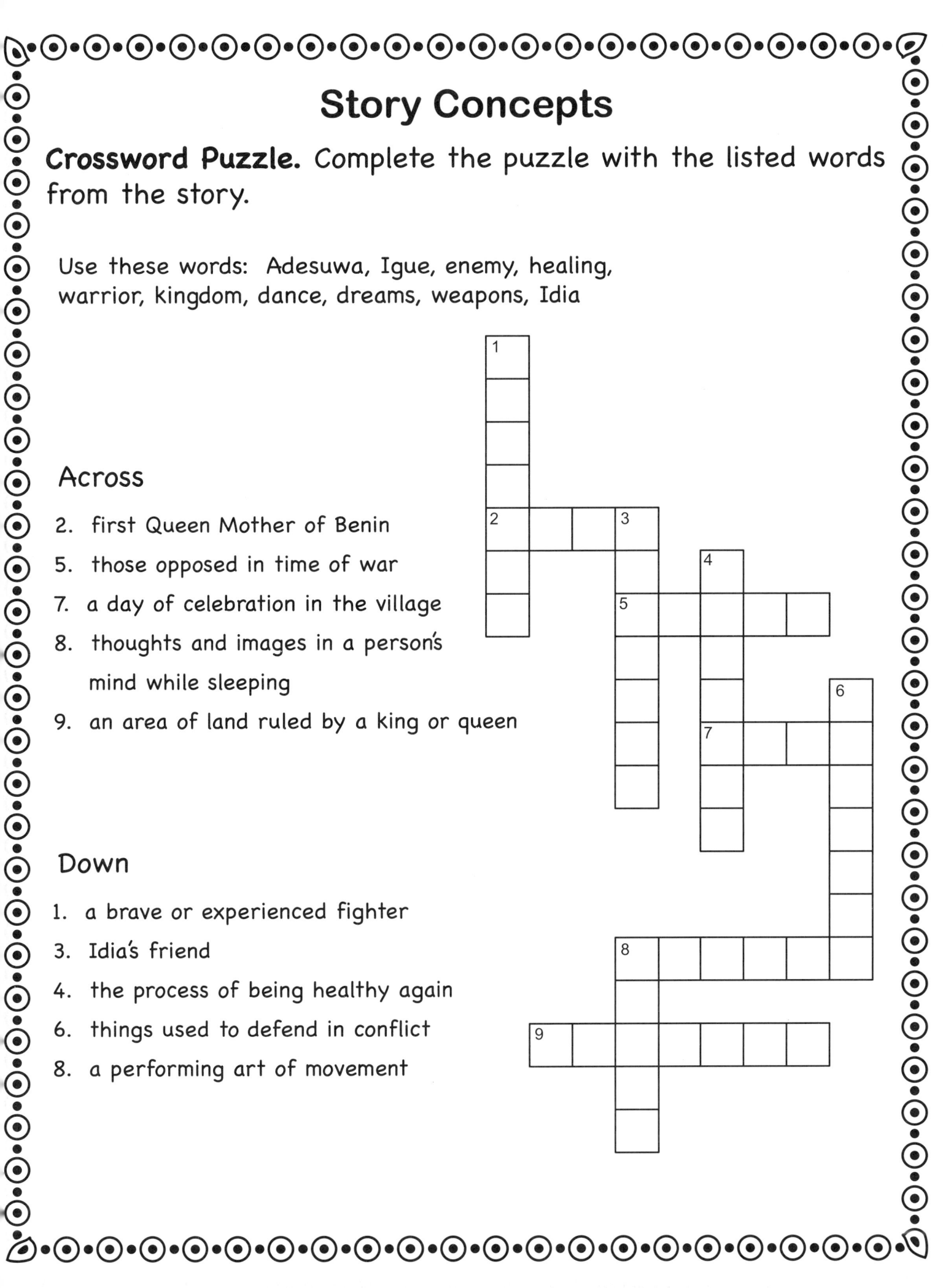

Story Concepts

Creative Expression: Answer the questions about the story in complete sentences.

1. Why were Idia and her friend Adesuwa so excited to attend the festival?

2. Why do you think Idia's father wanted her to keep dancing?

3. What role did the doctor play in the story?

4. How did Idia prepare to be the first woman to fight for the Benin Kingdom?

5. If you could choose a different title for the story, what would it be?

Journal Writing

Creative Writing: Draw and color a picture about the topics.

Optional: Add words or sentences to describe your pictures.

My day at a festival	A dream that came true
A time that I asked for help	Ways that I can help others

Story Words

Crossword Puzzle. Complete the puzzle with the listed words from the story.

Use these words: dream, dance, king, queen, friend, war, healing, warrior, Idia, kingdom

Across

2. movement
4. fight
5. male ruler
6. female ruler
8. a thought when sleeping
9. Queen Mother of Benin

Down

1. helping to get better
3. Adesuwa
5. land
7. Fighter

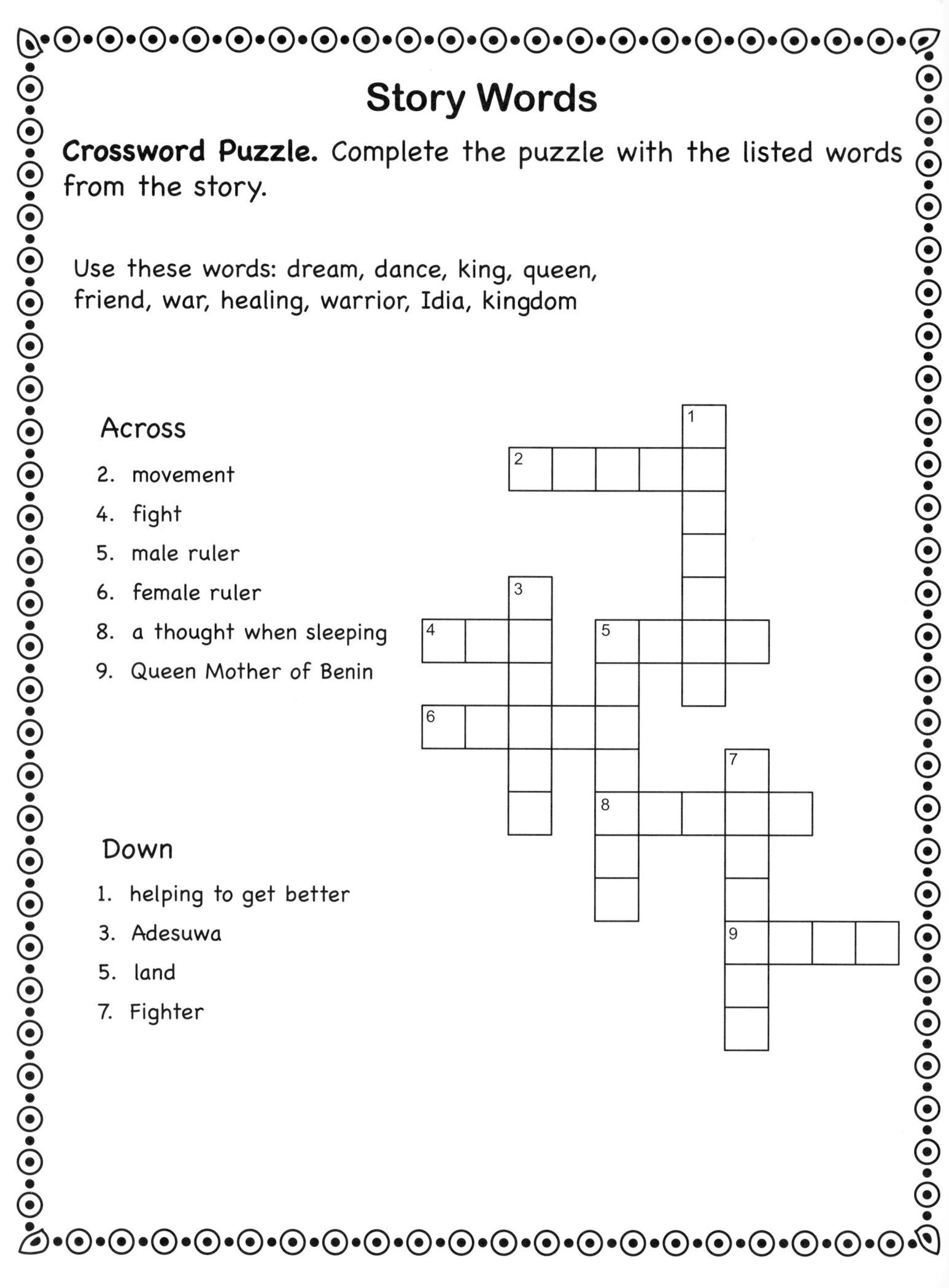

Understanding Characters

Matching. Which actions did the main characters do? Draw lines from the actions to the characters.
(Some of the characters have 2 answers.)

1. Idia

2. Adesuwa

3. Father

4. Mother

5. The young king (Oba)

6. The doctor

a. shared knowledge of being a warrior

b. had a repeating dream

c. was a village elder and encouraged Idia to dance

d. taught medicine and magic

e. skipped and laughed with Idia

f. wanted to marry Idia

g. eager to learn about war and healing

h. chanted prayers for protection and wisdom

I Have... Who Has?

Put the cards in order to complete the game!

Cut out the cards on the lines, scramble them up,
and see if you can answer all of the questions.
The first card begins with: "I have the first card."

I have the first card. Who has the role that Father played in the village?	I have village elder. Who has a question that Idia asked her father?
I have "Why must we have war?" Who has the day of celebration in the village?	I have Igue festival. Who has what Idia dreamed of?
I have a woman fighting in battle. Who has the fun that the girls looked forward to at the festival?	I have food, music, and dancing. Who has what Mother taught her daughter?
I have medicine, healing, and about the Gods. Who has what the young king admired?	I have energy, confidence, and rhythm of the dancers. Who has the person that gave wisdom and special prayers?
I have the doctor. Who has what was in the dream?	I have a queen. Who has the deity Idia's father said gave her her dreams?
I have Osanobua (God). Who has the title given to the first woman fighter for the kingdom?	I have the first Queen Mother of Benin. I have the last card.

Idia's Mask

Connect the dots. Idia's son Esigie loved her so much that he made specials masks and sculptures of her image.

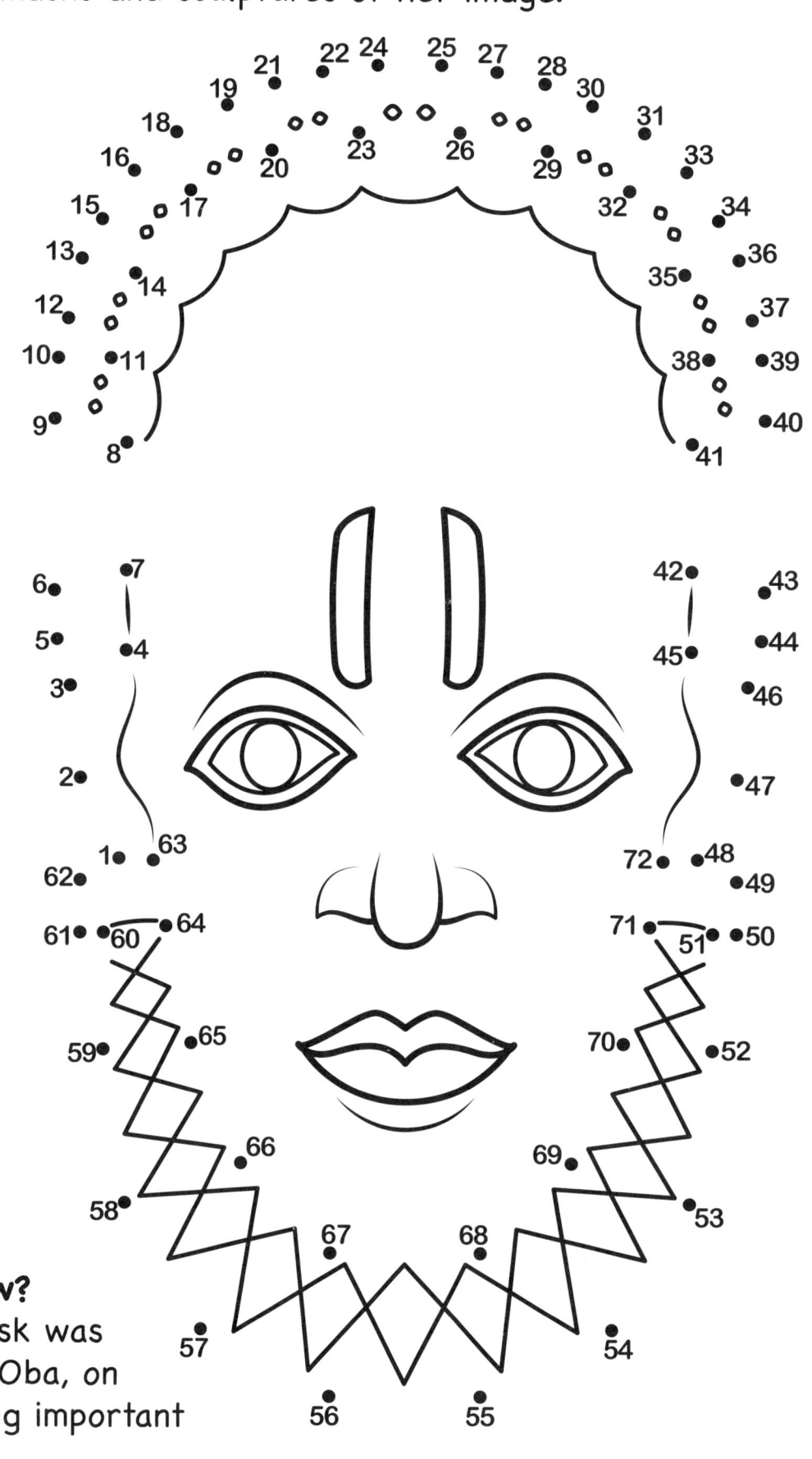

Did you know?
The ivory mask was worn by the Oba, on the hip, during important ceremonies.

The Benin Kingdom

Read the text below to help complete the puzzle on the next page.

The Benin Kingdom is located in part of what is now Nigeria, on the continent of Africa. The villagers since the 12th century spent much of their time farming the area and also making crafts like carving in wood and bronzes (metal sculptures). They traded their products (pepper, ivory, and even slaves) with the Portuguese and the British. The villagers lived in smaller villages which made up the empire.

The Benin Kingdom was ruled by a dynasty, so within the family, the role of leader was usually passed down from the king and queen to their son, and so on. The Benin people believed in animism, a belief that animals have souls. They also believed in many gods and supernatural power.

To protect the kingdom, a large wall was built from 800 - mid-1400 A.D. Over the course of 600 years, the villagers helped to build the wall. It took about 150 million hours of labor to build such a long wall of 16,000 km. They added a moat around the wall to keep out invaders. The wall had ramparts, broad-topped walls with a walkway and a stone parapet (a low protective wall along the edge of the main wall).

Eventually, the British overtook Benin in February, 1897, and became rulers. Because there were no written books at this time, stories were told about early African life and passed down orally from generation to generation. These are called oral traditions. That is how we know about the Benin Kingdom today. And now, we can share what we know in written format such as in books so that you can learn even more.

Which word doesn't belong?

Puzzle: Cross off one word on each row that does not belong. Write how the words are alike on each line.

1. Benin Kingdom   Nigeria   ~~North America~~

   The story takes place in the Benin Kingdom which is now part of Nigeria.

2. farmers   bankers   craftsmen

   _____

3. suburbs   villages   empire

   _____

4. Scottish   British   dynasty

   _____

5. queens   kings   presidents

   _____

6. storytelling   books   oral traditions

   _____

7. animism power   human strength   supernatural

   _____

8. carved wood   bronzes   watercolor paintings

   _____

9. pepper   ivory   apples

   _____

10. wire   moat   rampart

    _____

Bonus:

Can you think of a group of words about the text Idia of the Benin Kingdom? Cross off the one word that doesn't exist and write how the words are alike on the line.

_____

Traditional Rulers of Edo State

Finding Differences Puzzle. Circle the 10 differences between the puzzles.

Research Famous Walls

Find information about famous walls.

Walls have been used since ancient times for various reasons. They have marked borders between land areas. They also kept out unwanted people and protected the kingdom or settlement. The Benin Wall may not be as famous as the Great Wall of China, the Western Wall in Jerusalem, or the Berlin Wall that separated East and West Germany. But at one time in history, it was the largest man-made structure in the world! It was four times longer than the Wall of China, and more than 100 times the amount of materials than the Great Pyramid of Cheops were used to construct it.

Now it's time to research these walls and fill in the table below.

Name of Wall	When Built	How Long it Took to Build	Length of Wall
Benin Wall			
Great Wall of China			
Berlin Wall			

The Empires of Africa

Map Work. Color the ancient regions of Africa. Locate the Benin Empire.

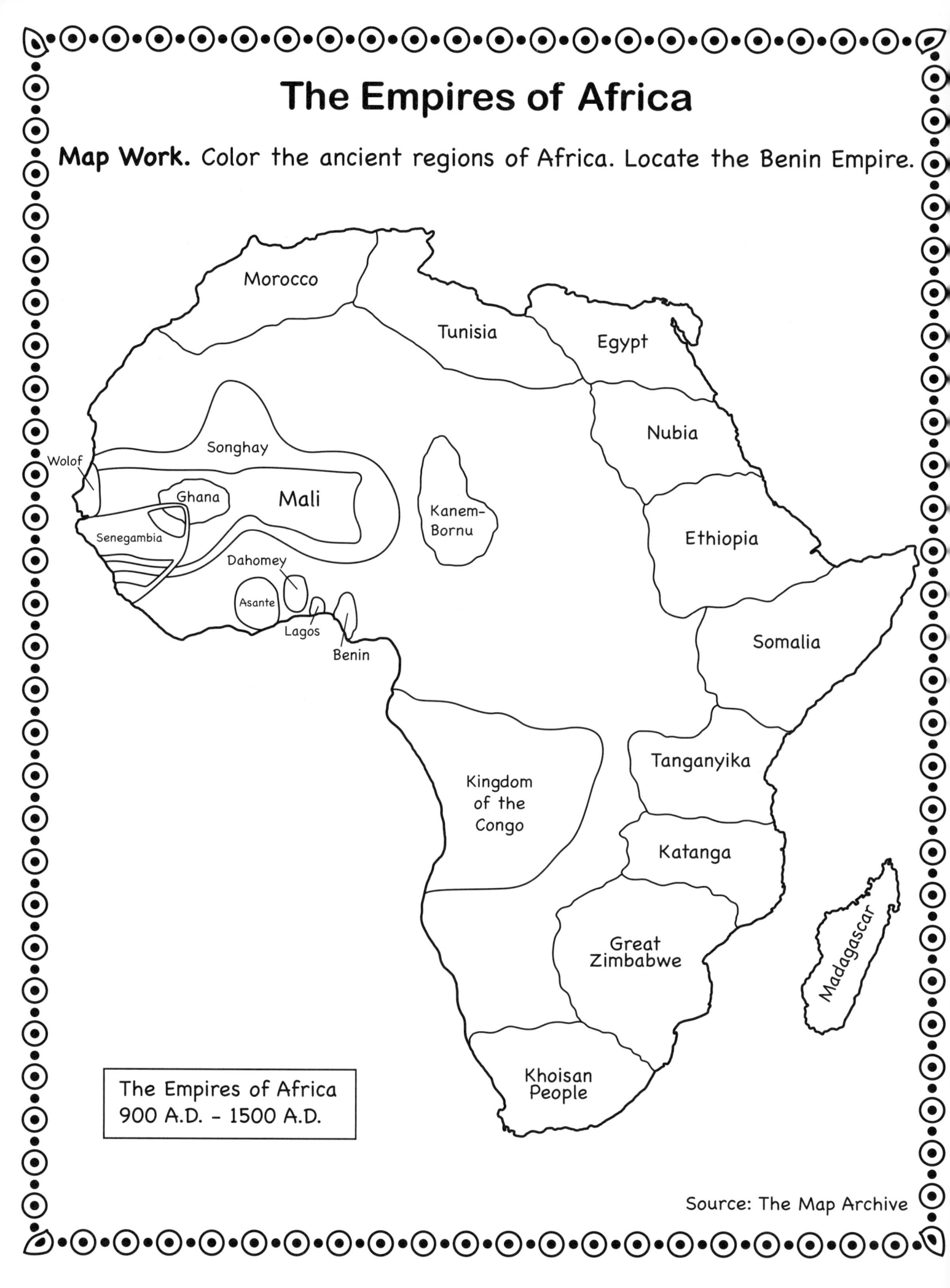

The Empires of Africa
900 A.D. - 1500 A.D.

Source: The Map Archive

The Countries of Africa

Making Comparisons. Study the map on the previous page. What differences can you find? Make a list in the box below.

Did you know?
The Republic of Benin is not the same as the Kingdom of Benin (now Edo State in Nigeria).

20th Century - Present

ANSWER KEY

The Edo Language - Word Puzzle
1. Oba, 2. Ema, 3. Ehra, 4. Iye, 5. Osanobua, 6. Ehi, 7. Iyoba

The Edo Language - Crossword Puzzle
Across: 1. erha, 3. iye, 5. osanobua, 8. iyoba
Down: 1. ehi, 4. ema, 6. oba, 7. uvbi

Story Words - Hidden Word Puzzle

Story Concepts - Crossword Puzzle
Across: 2. Idia, 5. enemy, 7. Igue, 8. dreams, 9. kingdom
Down: 1. warrior, 3. Adesuwa, 4. healing, 6. weapons, 8. dance

Story Concepts - Creative Expression
(Accept reasonable answers. The students should use complete sentences.)
1. Idia and Adesuwa were excited to attend the festival because they liked music, dancing, and the food. It would be lots of fun to see people and friends, etc.
2. Idia's father wanted her to dance because it is something she enjoyed and she was good at it.
3. The doctor said special prayers for protection for Idia. He also gave her two tribal marks on her forehead.
4. Idia learned war tactics from her father. He taught her about battle plans, how to deal with the enemy, and how to handle weapons. She also learned about the gods and medicine from her mother.
5. (Free expression)

Story Words - Crossword Puzzle
Across: 2. dance, 4. war, 5. king, 6. queen, 8. dream, 9. Idia
Down: 1. healing, 3. friend, 5. kingdom, 7. warrior

Understanding Characters - Matching
1. b,g   2. e   3. a,c   4. d   5. f   6. h

ANSWER KEY

Idia's Mask - Connect the dots

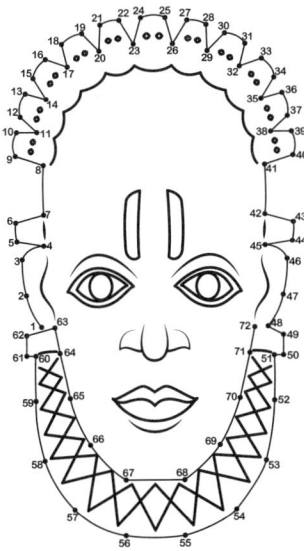

Which Word Doesn't Belong - Puzzle

(Accept reasonable answers.)

1. The story takes place in the Benin Kingdom in Nigeria. (cross off North America)
2. During this time period, villagers worked as farmers and craftsmen. (cross off bankers)
3. Villages made up the empire. (cross off suburbs)
4. The British and the dynasty ruled over Benin. (cross off Scottish)
5. Queens and kings ruled the kingdom. (cross off presidents)
6. Storytelling and oral traditions were ways to pass on stories. (cross off books)
7. Animism and supernatural power are similar beliefs. (cross off human strength)
8. The villagers carved wood and made bronzes as art forms. (cross off watercolor paintings)
9. The Benin Kingdom traded pepper and ivory. (cross off apples)
10. A large moat and ramparts were built around the city of Benin. (cross off wire)

Bonus: (Accept reasonable answers.)

Traditional Rulers of Edo State - Finding Differences Puzzle

Research Famous Walls

(Accept reasonable answers)

Benin Wall 800 AD—mid 1400; 150 million hours or 600 years; 16,000 km, about 9,942 miles

Great Wall of China 770-476 BC, 221-206 BC, 1368-1644; over 22 centuries; approx. 21,000 km or 13,000 miles

Berlin Wall 1961; 2 weeks; 111.9 km or 69.5 miles

This activity book accompanies our "Idia of the Benin Kingdom" picture book.

Head over to www.our-ancestories.com to grab your copy.

Our Ancestories

www.our-ancestories.com
contact@our-ancestories.com

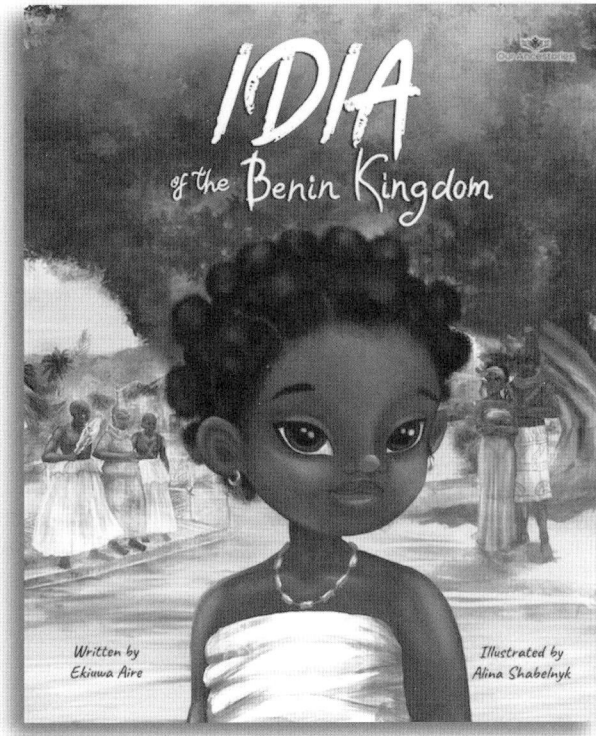

Get the entire collection, comprehensive teacher guides and more at
www.our-ancestories.com

IDIA OF THE BENIN KINGDOM STICKERS

IDIA OF THE BENIN KINGDOM STICKERS